Marketing secrets

The experts tell all!

D0306633

About the author

Peter Spalton CMC has spent the last 30 years in marketing. He has held senior marketing positions in ICL, Ericsson and Nokia. For the past 20 years he has worked as a freelance marketing consultant for multinationals, private companies, family businesses and public bodies. He is now a mentor and coach to chief executives and sales directors throughout the UK.

Collins
A division of HarperCollins*Publishers*
77-85 Fulham Palace Road, London W6 8JB

www.BusinessSecrets.net

First published in Great Britain in 2010 by HarperCollins*Publishers*
Published in Canada by HarperCollins*Canada*. www.harpercollins.ca
Published in Australia by HarperCollins*Australia*. www.harpercollins.com.au
Published in India by HarperCollins*PublishersIndia*. www.harpercollins.co.in

1

Copyright © HarperCollins*Publishers* 2010

Peter Spalton asserts the moral right to be identified as the author of this work.

A catalogue record for this book is available from the British Library.

ISBN 978-0-00-732811-6

Printed and bound at Clays Ltd, St Ives plc

Contents

Marketing covers all parts of your business

Most people think that marketing is mainly about advertising. A salesperson might regard marketing people as those who do the brochures and look after the website. But both views are only part of the picture, because marketing actually covers almost every aspect of a business.

I've been in marketing for 30 years and have worked as a brand manager, marketing director and freelance consultant in almost every type and size of business. And I've discovered that, although theory underpins what we all do, marketing is about innovation and the ability to learn from one's mistakes.

This book has some classic marketing theory written in an easy way. I have split it into seven chapters with 50 **secrets** that cover all the practical aspects of marketing. You must read them all, even if you think they're not all relevant to you. Be inquisitive and see what marketing people do elsewhere. Open your mind and ask yourself how each **secret** could work in your business.

■ **Marketing is a philosophy.** You must get yourself into the habit of thinking like a marketing person. Open your mind and imagine how you could seduce your customers and outwit your competition.

■ **Identify markets.** Everything starts with the customers and you must understand what makes them tick. To do this you need to be a bit of a clairvoyant and a psychologist, and to learn from experience.

■ **Create what people want.** At the end of the day someone must buy something, otherwise you have no reason to be in business. You must create what people want so they will choose you above your competitors.

■ **Look where people buy.** These days people don't just buy from a shop or a salesperson. You must make sure that they can get your product wherever they would expect it to be available.

■ **Devise your promotional mix.** There are literally hundreds of ways to promote your business and products. You must pick the tool that's right for the customer at each stage of the buying process.

■ **Get on the Internet.** You don't need to be an Internet expert or be able to program a computer. But you must have an open mind and the imagination to see what the Internet could do for your business.

■ **Make an achievable plan.** At some point someone will ask you to write down what you're going to do and why. Planning is rarely fun, but it helps you to clarify your thinking and justify what you intend to do.

When you've read these 50 **secrets** you'll know more about marketing than anyone else in your organization. Then again, I've been in marketing for 30 years and I'm still learning!

Marketing starts with your customer and ends in profit.

Marketing is a philosophy

Marketing is much more than just advertising or PR. It's a culture, a way of doing things that starts with a potential customer and ends up with a profit. In the middle are your competitors who are after the same customers and same profits. Your job, as a marketing person, is to use some proven tools and techniques to attack the competition and gain the customers. It's about predicting the future and using your imagination.

1.1

Marketing is about customers

If you pick up any of the classic books on marketing, you'll find a definition that goes something like this. "Marketing is the process where a company satisfies customer needs with a product and service at a price that generates a profit."

But marketing can be seen simply in two parts. Firstly, you must be able to work out what your customers want, now and in the future, and design a product and service that they will buy. Secondly, you must be able to tell potential customers all about your products and convince them to part with their money.

So a marketing person needs a mix of analysis, guesswork and psychology. It also helps if you are creative, but that's not essential, as you can pay someone else for creativity. Over the years, marketing people have devised some tools and techniques to help them think it all through. Traditionally they are known as the **four Ps of marketing**.

1 **Product.** You must be able to answer three questions about your product or service. Is it what customers want? How does it stack up against the competition? And when will it be out of date?

> **"The aim of marketing is to know and understand the customer so well that the product or service fits him or her and sells itself"**

Peter F. Drucker, management guru

2 **Price.** What someone will pay is always a judgement, especially if you are the first in the market. It's always better to price higher than you might initially think because you can always cut prices, whereas it's almost impossible to increase them later.

3 **Place.** This is the marketing term for where your customer buys your product. These days, it can be very complicated, incorporating a variety of shop sizes and types, the Internet and mail order. You must manage all those different outlets, or places, so you don't miss an opportunity to sell your products.

4 **Promotion.** There's not much point in creating a product if nobody has heard about it. There are two vital questions. How will customers find out about our products? And will they have enough information to make a decision?

Fifty years ago, a company made a product and people bought it. Thirty years ago, companies had to sell their products. Today, companies must market their brand successfully, so that people trust them before they buy their products.

You must continuously evolve your products and services to match the changing needs of your customers.

1.2

Marketing is definitely not selling

Many people are confused by the difference between sales and marketing. Just remember that marketing people deal with markets that contain many potential customers, and they talk to them as a group. Whereas salespeople deal with a few customers and talk to them one at a time.

There is a lot of overlap between the two roles and this can sometimes cause conflict and misunderstanding. But it is essential that marketing and sales people work together and support each other to achieve the organization's business objectives.

one minute wonder Make sure that you involve sales and customer service people as early as possible in all promotional campaigns. This eliminates hostility, misunderstanding and any feelings of things not being invented here.

■ **Marketing looks at what's happening in the market.** It's important to assess market trends and the competition. These days, most forward-thinking marketing people also involve salespeople to help their understanding. This is because salespeople have an intimate knowledge of individual customers and competitors.

■ **Marketing creates promotional campaigns.** This is to increase awareness of the business and its brand. Salespeople must be told what the promotions are doing and when they're going to happen. Then sales can ride on the back of the campaign and generate additional business.

■ **Marketing prepares promotional material.** This is to help potential customers understand what your business does. It includes brochures, presentations and your website. Salespeople should use these to describe the business and explain the benefits of your products to individual customers.

■ **Marketing works with sales.** Together they create campaigns to generate enquiries from customers. It is essential that these campaigns support sales activities and objectives.

■ **Sales weeds out the time-wasters.** Sales must identify those potential customers who are seriously interested in buying your products. It's also their job to convince individual customers to make a purchase. Then salespeople will either take an order or the money.

■ **Sales and marketing work together on catalogues.** Whether it's with mail order, over the Internet or through third parties such as distributors and agents, marketing and sales must work together. In this situation marketing must support sales.

To learn more about selling, you should read the *Selling Secrets* book in this series.

Marketing approaches broad groups of potential customers; salespeople talk to them individually.

1.3

Adapt and adopt, learn and evolve

Marketing people love change because it means opportunity. Markets, the competition and technology never stand still, and you must embrace this culture of constant change. Those businesses that didn't have been forgotten.

Can you name any company that used to make slide rules or steam cars? The crossbow was destroyed by the musket, the musket by the rifle, and the rifle by who knows what.

The best marketing people understand that they can't stand still because the world does not stand still. Their philosophy is one that embraces change with open arms. If you want to be successful in marketing, you'll need to do the same. That means never being satisfied with the way things are, but instead constantly looking at how things could be improved, particularly in relation to the competition.

one minute wonder See what happens when you buy your main competitor's product. Was it easy? How was their service compared to yours? If you're not ahead, you need to change.

"Marketing takes a day to learn. Unfortunately it takes a lifetime to master" Philip Kotler, marketing guru

■ **Always keep an eye on your competition.** Regularly look at what your competitors are up to. Analyse what they're good at and what they're not. Adjust your own approach and play to their weak spots.

■ **Buy your competitors' products.** You must buy their products and give them to your design people. Ask them what's good and what's bad about them. Try to understand what they're doing now and predict what they're going to do next year and the year after.

■ **See what's happening in your industry in other countries.** Some countries are way ahead of others. See what they're up to because it's where your market might be in two, three or five years' time.

■ **Look at other industries and see how they do things.** Adapt their successful ways to your business. Most companies in the same industry do things in a similar way. So a different approach may give you a unique advantage over your competitors.

■ **Attend seminars and workshops.** Go to at least two workshops a year on sales and marketing. Network with the audience and find out what works well for them. Even if you don't learn anything, you'll remember something good that you'd forgotten.

■ **Regularly review your own performance.** Don't be afraid to admit that something didn't work as well as you'd hoped. Remember, it's always better to do something, than regret doing nothing.

The secret of success in marketing is to keep learning and evolving the way that you do things.

Change means opportunity. Embrace it and try new things.

1.4

Customers need to be seduced

Fifty years ago people went to the local shops for most of what they needed. The shopkeeper knew them and took time to talk and ask about their family. In those days, shopping was relaxed and shopkeepers were usually friendly.

Gradually, though, the small local shops disappeared as the large chains and supermarkets took over. Shopping then became impersonal. It became transaction-based: you went to a shop, bought what you needed and left. As it didn't really matter where you shopped, you weren't loyal to any particular retail outlet. After all, you could get your favourite brands anywhere. But, at the start of this century, companies realized that they needed to engage with their customers to keep them coming back. Loyalty, lifestyles and aspirations became the buzzwords of the day in marketing.

■ **The Apple example.** In the early 1990s, Apple was a small, specialist computer company. Its customers were loyal and most of them worked in the fashion, design and media industries. But, in October 2001, the company launched the iPod, which was aimed at young people. It became a lifestyle purchase and a statement of freedom.

Two years later, the company introduced iTunes, which added a recurring revenue stream. Within seven years Apple had sold 150 million units and transformed the company and the entire music business.

■ **The Emirates example.** In the 1980s airlines were totally transaction based. If you wanted to fly, you bought a ticket and that was it. But Emirates broke the mould when it decided to sell the sensuous experience of flying. They changed their slogan to "Fly Emirates, keep discovering", and put their 16,000 cabin staff in designer uniforms. With minimum cost, they dramatically increased the perceived value of flying Emirates. Since then, the company has won 400 industry awards.

■ **The Red Bull example.** In 1987, a European company launched a sports drink called Red Bull. Its marketing was aggressive and it sponsored sports and extreme activities: Formula 1 racing, snowboarding, surfing, skateboarding and windsurfing. It is clearly aimed at young men and now produces a monthly magazine called the Red Bulletin, available online, and free in many bars, clubs and hotels. With its memorable slogan, "Red Bull gives you Wings", today the company sells more than 3 billion cans a year around the world.

All these companies have one thing in common. They've each found out how to seduce their customers effectively. You must learn how to do the same. It starts by clearly understanding what you do and what you want your customers to feel about you. Find out more about this in Secrets 2.2 and 5.10.

Learn to seduce your customers so that they keep wanting you.

Identify markets

Your market is vital. It's the group of potential customers who will use your type of product. So you must understand who will buy your product, why they will buy it and how they will make the decision. This is where you need to be part psychic, part psychologist. You also need to realize that marketing is like warfare, and you will probably need to use guerilla tactics. This means you must spot opportunities and attack little bits of the market, one at a time.

2.1

Find a gap in the market

Do you start with a product, an idea or a skill? Whatever your answer, you must find a gap in the market to focus on. You're not likely to succeed if you go head on against a business that is already established. You must find a group of potential customers that the main players have ignored.

Think about how Nintendo spotted a gap in the crowded market for computer game consoles. It chose families, rather than teenage boys, and the Wii has become one of the marketing success stories of the last few years. A gap in the market is called a niche. It must be large enough for you to make a reasonable profit and small enough for you to dominate it.

case study AT Cross is famous for its gold-plated writing instruments that every up-and-coming executive wants to have. Rather than attacking the whole stationery market, and making

■ **Product niche.** Your product could have a unique feature that appeals to a particular market group or application. Dyson's Cyclone vacuum cleaner is an example of this type.

■ **Location niche.** This is usually a service, such as a local convenience store that's open all hours, or an airport departure lounge shop.

■ **Customer niche.** Find a group of potential customers that have similar characteristics or interests that you can easily identify. The grey market, for example, refers to people over 60. Extreme sport enthusiasts form another market niche.

■ **Low price niche.** You could decide to reduce the quality or the number of your product's features and sell it at a reduced price. This is what the food suppliers do with their 'own-label' products.

■ **Luxury niche.** You can price yourself into a market with a high quality, stylish and expensive product. The most important aspect of this niche is to have the right image and reputation. Honda created a new brand, Lexus, to move into the luxury niche. It also built a new dealer network to distance itself from the existing Honda brand.

If you already sell a product in a particular market niche, you need to see if there are any other niches where it would also sell. Often you can make a simple modification and sell it into another group of customers. There's more about this in Secret 3.4

You must find a niche in the market, without too much competition, where you will sell enough to make a profit.

every sort of pen and pencil imaginable, it has chosen to focus on the high-price niche, and has added business bags and gold-plated accessories, such as cuff links, to its exclusive product range.

2.2

Define your ideal customer

The work that you do to define your potential customer is probably the most valuable time you spend in marketing. Traditional marketing people call this segmentation, and they will put a lot of time and energy into getting it right.

Let's assume that you have an idea for a product and need to decide who it's aimed at. The best way to do this is to have a meeting with two or three people who know the product and the type of customers you're interested in, then take these four simple steps.

1 **Start with demographics.** If you are selling to consumers, this is their age, gender, income bracket and geographic location. If you sell to businesses, it's their size, industry and the region or country in which they are based.

> **case study** In the 1950s, Parker turned the pen business on its head when it decided that its ideal customer was someone looking for a gift. Parker Pens put more money into the packaging, so their

2 **Look at buying habits.** Will customers be heavy users and buy your products and services every day, week or month? Or will they buy only once every few years? For example, office workers in the city may buy coffee from the same place every day, whereas, at the other extreme, people tend to buy a car only every few years and a house just three or four times in their life.

3 **Consider who will purchase the product.** And how they will pay for it. For example, baby clothes are for babies but they're bought by parents, grandparents and friends. Will people pay for your product with cash or credit card? Or, in the case of a very expensive item, will they need a bank loan? If so, you might like to approach a bank so that you can arrange loans on behalf of your customers. That would be a great added-value service.

4 **Think about the motives for buying your products.** Is it a lifestyle purchase, where customers buy to feel good or improve their status in their community? Or will they buy to solve a problem, save time or reduce costs? And think about whether they will make a decision based on quality, service or price.

When you have finished, you should have a picture of your ideal customer. Then you need to consider how they might find out about you, where they would buy your products and the size of the market.

The time you spend on clearly defining your ideal customer is never wasted.

products became presents. These days, we have specific pens for pre-school children, school children, students, office workers and professionals. And nobody actually buys a pen for themselves.

2.3

Understand how and why they buy

This is where you need to be a bit of a psychologist. There are two aspects to this. You have to understand why people would want to buy your type of product. And, you must know why they would choose yours rather than one of your competitor's.

Think for a moment about what people actually do before they part with their money. Whether you realize it or not, they think through four steps, usually without knowing it. We call these the buying stages.

■ **Need or want stage.** This is when a person decides that they want or need something. It might be that they want to save money or time, or they might want to gain something, such as money or status. Equally, they might want to avoid something, such as hunger, thirst or having to clean the house on their hands and knees.

■ **Knowledge stage.** They search for information to help them decide which one to buy. For some products, they will look at advertising, brochures or reviews in specialist magazines. For other, more basic products, such as bread, they'll probably just look at them on the shelf.

"Look at markets through the other end of the telescope – not the lens of what you want to sell, but the lens of what people want to buy"

Gary Bencivenga, American celebrity copywriter

■ **Preference stage.** Then they actually make a decision and choose the one they will have. Even though they might have thoroughly researched the product, they will often subconsciously decide on things like colour, quality, price, style or what's in fashion.

■ **Buy and justify stage.** After they have made their decision and bought the product, they will then justify to themselves that they've made the right choice. They will say things like "it was the best," or "it was reduced in price".

Some people make almost instant decisions because they're known as decisive. Some need lots of information and facts before they can make a decision. They are methodical and they just need time. Then there is another group, who take almost forever to make a decision. These are cautious and you will need to encourage them to make the decision by telling them who else has bought your product.

In Secret 5.3 you will see which sort of advertising and promotion you must do for each stage of the buying process.

You need to be a bit of a psychologist to see how people make a decision and why they would buy your product.

2.4

Look at who really makes the decisions

If you're alone and want a sandwich or coffee, the decision is fairly easy. But, unfortunately, most purchases involve many people, especially if it's a product or service for a business.

Even something that at first sight appears to be simple can involve more than one person. Imagine a mother in the shopping mall with her two children. One of them says, "I want a sweet." That child is known as the initiator and is also the consumer. The mother is the buyer. The other child has a vested interest in the decision because they know that they'll get a sweet too. That child is a stakeholder. If the purchase is not a sweet but something more expensive, the other parent may be involved in the decision process also. We give the people these names to help explain their role in the decision process of making a purchase.

■ **Initiator.** The person who first suggests the idea. In the example above, this is one of the children. If the mother had made the suggestion by asking, "Would you like a sweet?", she'd be in initiator instead.
■ **Consumer.** The person who actually uses the product or service. This is the child in the example above. But, if you wanted to buy a computer network for a business, it might be a whole team of people.

"Most sales are lost because the salesman presented his product before he knew what motivated everyone else involved"

Gary Bencivenga, American celebrity copywriter

■ **Influencer.** A person or group of people whose views and advice have a bearing on the buying decision. In the example of buying sweets, this could be a dentist who might suggest that sweets are bad for the teeth.

■ **Money man/woman.** The person who has the money or signs the cheque. They have the ultimate authority to say, "No, we can't afford it".

■ **Buyer.** The person who actually buys or pays for the product or service. In business these are the people who check the contract and look at the viability of the supplier in the long term.

■ **Stakeholder.** A person or group of people who have no influence over the decision, but are interested in the purchase.

The more expensive the product, the more people you'll tend to find involved in the decision. You must identify the individuals by name and work with your salespeople to make sure that you influence them correctly. It's the little things that matter, so you must give the right kind of information to the right person. For example, the buyer is not interested in the technical merit of your product, they are interested in the status of your company. The money man is really only interested in making sure that they get value for money.

Purchases are never as simple as they seem, and there can be many people involved in even an easy decision.

2.5

Know your strengths and weaknesses

The best marketing people know exactly what they're good at, and what they're not so good at – their strengths and weaknesses. You also need to have an understanding of the strengths and weaknesses of your competitors, and know what your customers think of you and your products.

Your customers' views are much more important than your own. I'm sure you think that you have the best products in the world, but actually it's their perception that matters most. And you must match your product and customer service to their expectations, based on your marketing material.

one minute wonder Phone your customers immediately after they have bought something from you. You will then get their instant reaction to how the purchase went.

■ **Product.** Ask customers how the features, quality and reliability of your product stacked up to what they had expected.

■ **Price.** Did they feel that they got value for money? Find out if they got more or less than they had expected.

■ **Availability.** How easy was it for them to find out the information they needed when choosing which product to buy? How easy was it for them to buy it? Was it in stock?

■ **Service.** What did they think of your service? Was it friendly, efficient and did it match what they had anticipated?

Many businesses employ someone to phone customers; others use the post. A postal or email survey can gather more information, but it won't capture the customer's immediate feelings.

You also need to talk to your prospective customers, particularly those who have never purchased anything from you. Ask them if they've heard about your business and what they think you stand for. This is called your company's level of awareness.

Make a list of what you think you're good at and a list of what you're not so good at, and add your customers' views to the lists. Then look long and hard at each of the weaknesses, and work out how you can address them. Ideally, you want to turn them around completely, so that they become strengths.

Know what you're good at and not so good at, so you can play to your strengths and fix your weaknesses.

2.6

Define your proposi-
tion and values

Once people have decided that they want to buy something, they tend to choose the business that closely matches their own lifestyle and values. You need to define what you do and what you stand for as a business.

You need a very clear statement that is called your proposition. If you're not a household name it needs to say what you do. If you are a well-known brand you can get away with a slogan, such as "We try harder", from Avis, or "The ultimate driving experience", from BMW.

At first sight, it seems very difficult to create your proposition and brand values. But your proposition should just say clearly what you do in one sentence. One way is to fill the gaps in this statement: we supply (customers) with (product) that will (benefit). For example, "We supply commercial vehicle manufacturers and repairers in South America with cooling systems that will cope with the rugged conditions and harsh climate".

Your brand values are what you want your customers to feel when they see and interact with your business. You need to match these to your market, though. For example, it's no good trying to be a young and energetic business if your market is elderly people.

one minute wonder Visit the food shops in your area and look at their displays. What colours do they use? What's the layout like? What sort of people shop there? Try to decide what their brand values are, and which is their target group of customers.

Think which one of these best describes your business. And is it what your target customers want?

■ **Reliable and stable.** The banks and insurance companies must come across as safe and secure.

■ **Exciting and energetic.** BMW and Red Bull have created energetic brands with emotional appeal.

■ **Innovative and leading edge.** Brands like Audi, Apple and Sony promote their leading-edge technology.

■ **Creative and stylish.** Think about Gucci and Ferrari.

■ **Sophisticated and high-status.** Brands such as Rolls Royce, Dunhill and Rolex say that you've arrived.

■ **Value for money.** Companies like Kia, Skoda, Hyundai and Asus Computers push value for money.

People today want to feel engaged with a company and be proud to buy its products. Your proposition and your brand values show this and form your promise to customers. Just make sure that you never break this bond of trust.

You must be able to state clearly what you do and what you stand for in fewer than 35 words.

2.7

Research your competitors

Every business has competitors. And actually it's good for everyone, as the combined spend on promotion and advertising increases the size and growth of the market. Only the very largest companies can hope to cover the whole market and all the niches within it. You must understand who your competitors are and how you stack up against them.

■ **Direct competitors.** These are businesses with whom you compete head to head in your target market. Although all of them are important, you've probably got only one or two key competitors. Those are the businesses that you're up against all the time.

■ **Other competitors.** These supply a similar product to your own, but in different parts of the market. Sometimes they are overseas companies, sometimes they sell into a different niche. You need to keep an eye on them, as they could easily move into your target market at any time.

■ **Indirect competitors.** These are not competitors in the usual sense of the word. They are other ways that your potential customers could spend their money rather than buying your product. For example, a new car is an indirect competitor to a holiday.

one minute wonder Set up a Google Alert for your business name and each of your competitors. Then you'll get an email every time they appear on the Internet, or they update their website or blog.

You must gather some basic information about each of your competitors in each of the top two categories opposite – direct and other competitors. Things like location, business size, website, product information and their target customer groups. Turn it into a rough guide to your competitors and send it to all your sales and marketing staff for them to add more information. Make it a living document that you update every couple of months.

For each of your key competitors you must spend time working out their strengths and weaknesses. Monitor their website every month and keep an eye open for them in the press. Little things like a job vacancy can tell you if they intend to expand into new areas. Try and work out what they're trying to achieve and where they are going. Ask yourself, what's their commitment to a particular product? Are they marketing it aggressively? Will they launch a new version? Try and guess how much they depend on a particular product or market. Is it a large slice of their sales revenue so they can't afford to lose it?

With questions like that, you can work out what they'll do over the next couple of years. And information is power.

Create a rough guide for each of your key competitors that looks at their strengths and weaknesses.

2.8

Analyse market trends and forces

Markets, customers, products and competitors never stand still. So you must look at what's happening in your market at least once a year.

Some of the things that affect your market are completely outside your control. These are known as macro forces and include things such as the economy, legislation, changes in government policy, political turmoil and wars. Ask yourself what would happen if…? Or what will happen when…?

You must also watch the other things that are happening in your market or industry. These are the micro forces. Whilst you can't control them, you can sometimes influence them. They include new products from your competitors, changes in customer attitudes and the development of new technology.

■ **Read your industry or trade press.** You must be up-to-date with what's going on. Subscribe to RSS feeds from the blogs of industry commentators and trend watchers.

■ **Check out government statistics.** These are often available on the Internet for your own country and others you wish to research.

"Marketing people... have come to rely too much on research, and they use it as a drunkard uses a lamppost for support, rather than for illumination" **David Ogilvy, British-born advertising guru**

■ **Attend exhibitions, trade shows and conferences.** This is a chance to talk to the people who have their ears to the ground to find out the latest industry gossip.

■ **Network with the people that influence your market.** The movers, shakers and trend setters who are ahead of most people can give you a good idea of what's going to happen next in your industry.

■ **Talk to your customers.** Your customers will probably know more about what's happening in their market than you do. You must get them together as a focus group and listen to their views on what's going on.

■ **Watch the leading edge customers.** It's so important to see what your competitors' customers are doing. The leading edge ones are the innovators. They buy the latest technology and set the market trends.

■ **Look at other similar industries.** You can learn so much if you look at markets that are similar to your own, particularly in the consumer field. Study the trends in other parts of the world and think about what you would do if a similar situation presented itself in your country and in your market.

Market trends and dynamics are all about what might happen in the future. Use your judgement to decide what you need to do now.

Markets and technologies never stand still, so you must aim to be ahead of the game rather than chase behind a trend.

2.9

Estimate market size and potential

This always seems the most difficult bit to begin with. But all you actually need to do is estimate the total size of your market and make an informed guess about its potential growth.

Sometimes this information has already been published in your industry press. If not, a market research company can sell it to you. Sometimes, however, you just have to do it yourself.

1 First we must estimate the total population of businesses or consumers in the market. These numbers are usually published in government statistics and business directories. The number of people and homes in a particular area is usually available on-line. And you can simply count the number of businesses of a particular type in the various trade directories. Or ask an industry association how many members they have. Let's assume that we want to sell non-electric toothbrushes for adults in Germany. There are 80 million adults in Germany, so the total market is 80 million consumers.

2 Then we need to guess how much of the total market will actually use our type of product in the foreseeable future. Germany is a developed country, and we can roughly guess, or find out, that 30% of the population use an electric toothbrush. This reduces our market to 56 million consumers.

3 Now we need to calculate how many times each consumer would buy our type of product. Let's say that a toothbrush lasts about a month so people would normally buy ten a year. This takes the market for non-electric toothbrushes in Germany to 560 million units per year. And, at $2 a time, it's worth over $1 billion per annum. The market growth, however, is limited by the birth rate.

4 Finally, you need to look at each of your competitors and estimate how many products of your type they sell in the market every year. But make sure that you compare like for like. In our example, it would be non-electric toothbrushes into Germany. If you have researched them well enough, you can often work it out from their accounts and the prices. Of course, you will have to guess the sales split between each of their products. But you can usually do that from the emphasis they place on each of them in their promotional activities.

When you've finished, you will have an estimate of the market share of all your competitors. If you want to enter the market, you must either find a gap or attack a weak competitor head on.

Looking at market size and growth is a combination of scientific research and pure guesswork.

Create what people want

Let's look at the first two 'P's of the classical marketing mix: product and price. Whether you market a product or a service, in the overall scheme of things, there's not much difference between them. They both satisfy a customer need and they both must be marketed in similar ways. In marketing terms, the packaging is the only real difference, and one of the things you must learn to do is package services so they become tangible. Everything else is the same.

3.1

Identify features and benefits

So you've created an amazing product and you're sure that everyone will want to buy it. You have detailed all your product's features, probably as a list of its specifications. However, it's only really technical people who actually make a purchase based on a list of specifications. What you need to do now is turn your features into advantages and benefits.

■ **An advantage is what your type of product does for the user.** For example, with a vacuum cleaner you can clean the house quicker and with less effort. But that is true of all vacuum cleaners.

> **case study** In 1986, James Dyson designed a vacuum cleaner that didn't have a dust bag, which meant that it never lost suction. All the existing manufacturers refused to license his technology. So he decided to make and sell the product himself. In 1999, US company Hoover was found guilty of

■ A benefit is what your product's feature does for the user.
You will have specific features that benefit the user. So if your vacuum cleaner has a mechanism to retract the cord, then the benefit is that it doesn't get tangled.

It's actually easy to work out your product's benefits. Look at each of its features in turn and complete the sentence: "Our product has (feature) which means that (benefit)" So, in the example above: "Our product has a retractable cord which means that it doesn't get tangled".

People actually decide which product to choose on its benefits. Although sometimes they will make an emotional decision based on what makes them feel good. Such as with shoes, perfumes and gadgets.

Some benefits are more important than others, so you must put them in an order of priority. And, as with most marketing judgements, you should ask your customers. This is called product sampling and is always done with foods to work out the flavours that customers prefer. So, take your list and ask a group of customers to tell you which are the most important benefits to them. Then ask them to pick out the top three or four, so you have an idea of messages you should use to sell the product. These are the "hot buttons" that you must use on on your promotional material and product packaging.

People don't buy features, they buy what the product will do for them.

patent infringement. Hoover also admitted that it had considered buying the patent from Dyson to keep the technology out of the market. In 2001, Dyson launched the product in the UK at a premium price, and, four years later, his company had sales worth over $300 million per annum.

3.2

Understand your competitive edge

Marketing people refer to what you are selling as your offering. It is usually a combination of a product and a service, and it mustn't be identical to your competitors'. If it is, you are only able to compete on price. And that's easy for a competitor to attack if they're willing to lose money in the short term to drive you out of business.

So you must work out what advantage you have over each of your competitors. This is called competitive advantage. This is important, as it's the reason why people will choose your product over another. It is, therefore, essential that you analyse your complete offering against each of your key competitors.

case study Viking Direct, the UK subsidiary of the US giant Office Depot, sells office consumables by mail order. To be different, it created a guaranteed next day delivery as it's competitive advantage. If it failed,

1 Make a list of the things that would make a customer choose your offering. Maybe it's your product quality and reliability. Maybe it's what people think about your brand.

2 Decide whether you are better, the same or worse than each of your competitors for each factor on your list. Be honest – it is unlikely that you'll be better than your competitors in all areas.

3 Pick the factors where you are obviously better, as these are what we call your competitive advantages. Look at those where you're not so good, and think how you could improve them.

If your competitive advantages relate to your product, you must keep an eye on your competition. Product advantages are fairly easy to copy. If they relate to your reputation or brand, though, it will take much longer for a competitor to catch up. And if you don't have any competitive advantages, you need to create some.

Customer service is one of the best areas to create advantage because it also increases your perceived value (see Secret 3.7). It can be copied by a competitor, although it needs people with the right skills.

Brand image and reputation is the most difficult advantage to create. It can take a lot of money and a long time to build a reputation. A technological advantage is always short lived because it's usually easy to copy, in spite of patents. And price is never a lasting advantage.

You're going nowhere if you haven't got any competitive advantages.

you got your order free. The do this, the company changed the staff hours so they started work at 11 am and finished at 9 pm. At 9:15 pm all the day's orders were dispatched by overnight courier.

3.3

Get the mix right to manage life cycles

Most modern businesses sell a mix of products and services to spread the risk and generate the best level of profit. Businesses with only one product always fail because products have a life cycle, like a butterfly. They start with an idea, then a prototype is made. The product comes to life and people buy it, but eventually it will be overtaken by technology and go into decline and death.

Consider the main difference between products and services. You make products, and they sit on a shelf until you sell them. If you don't sell one today, you can still sell it tomorrow. Whereas a service is time-based. If you don't sell a block of time, you can never sell it again. Nobody will buy yesterday's hotel room or buy a flight to New York that left last week. But there is one important similarity between them. They both have a lifespan. They're conceived, born and will eventually die.

■ **Design.** During the first stage, you must design a product that customers will want by the time you launch it. You must intercept future technology so that it's up-to-date when you launch it.

■ Introduction. In this stage, you will sell small quantities of your product to a small number of customers. During the introduction period, you must focus on product quality, as you don't want to be hit by lots of returns and future warranty costs.

■ Growth. This is when your product starts to take off. You must promote it heavily and make sure that it's in stock where customers will expect to find it.

■ Early maturity. At some point, your rate of growth will slow down. And, if you've been successful, other companies will begin to sell competitive products that are cheaper than your own. So, be ready to cut your price if necessary.

■ Maturity. Here, you need to control your sales and marketing costs to make the most profit. You also need to monitor sales, so that you are able to see the tipping point to the next stage.

■ Decline and death. At some point, your product will no longer be profitable. When that happens, you must make a hard decision and withdraw it from the market.

To be successful in business, you must have a product in each stage of the life cycle. Then you will always have a new product to replace an existing one, when it goes into decline. Car and mobile phone companies are masters of this strategy.

A single-product company dies when its product reaches the end of its life. You must have a mix of both old and new products to survive.

3.4

Bundle and unbundle

Each of your products should be aimed at a specific group of customers. But there will be other people in the market who would buy your product if it was slightly different. You must try and create new products from your current one in order to increase the number of potential customers.

You need to be imaginative and say things such as, "What would happen if we removed some of the features of the product?" Or, "What could we add to our product to make it different?" The computer industry is very good at this and many software programs come in a variety of versions.

■ **Free version.** An entry level product, with limited features and annoying adverts. It's aimed at casual users and those who want to try it. For a small price, you can remove the adverts and unlock more features.

case study Computer software manufacturers are adept at diversifying their product range by selling the same thing in different ways. Microsoft, for example, has put together three separate products, Word, Excel

■ Light version. This has additional features and no adverts. It's aimed at the self-employed person or home user. For an extra fee, you can unlock more features at any time.

■ Professional version. This is aimed at small businesses. It is more expensive than the light version and has even more features. You can either purchase it directly from the manufacturer, or upgrade from the light version.

■ Network version. This is the fully-featured product, and is aimed at larger businesses, which need to work across a network.

Many other companies, such as manufacturers of air-conditioning units and heating systems, start with a fully-featured product that they then cut down to create two more products: a basic version and a standard one. In a similar way, the car companies make 'limited edition' models by adding non-standard features and unusual paint finishes. These models are aimed at fashion-conscious people who want to show off their individual style.

Bundling and unbundling is an easy, quick and cheap way to produce new products. So, before a product leaves the growth stage, you must look at ways to bundle and unbundle it, and create new products before your competitors do.

Create bundled and unbundled products to sell to different sets of customers.

and Powerpoint, to create Microsoft Office, which costs just over the price of two of them. This is called bundling, and is really just a three-for-two deal to encourage you to spend more money.

3.5

Match perceived value and price

Price is one of the most difficult things to get right, especially if you've got a brand new product or service. It's much easier if there are already similar products on the market. Then all you need to do is decide whether you're going to be cheaper or more expensive. You must never ever have the same price as your nearest competitor.

The lower the price, the more you will sell. The higher the price, the less you will sell. You might decide to sell at a low price so you'll gain market share very quickly. This is called pricing for penetration. Alternatively, if your product is in short supply, you might decide to price for profit. This is called skimming the market.

 Find out the prices of all your competitors' products and list them in price order.

 Consider your competitive advantage (see Secret 3.2) and decide where you should place yourself on the list. Have you enough competitive advantage to justify that position?

one minute wonder If you want to increase your profits, just slightly increase your price. A 5–10% price increase probably won't affect your sales very much, and the increase will go straight to your bottom line.

3 Sometimes you might decide to go for a premium price. In other words, slightly more expensive than your nearest competitor on the list. Usually it's better to be slightly cheaper.

4 Check that you have got your price about right by asking potential customers. But be careful, because people will often lie or exaggerate when asked what they would be prepared to pay for a particular product.

5 Calculate what profit you will make when you sell your product at that price. If it's not enough, you need to add more value (see Secret 3.7).

You can also price yourself into a market. But your customer has to believe they're buying a quality or a rare product. This works particularly well in the fashion and beauty industries. There, it serves no purpose to have an expensive-looking perfume at a ridiculously cheap price. People just won't believe it. They will probably think that it's a fake, a con or a trick.

Remember that price is what the customer pays for your product, value is what they think it's worth. You must always make the value more than the price.

Price is nothing to do with cost. Price is about what the customer will pay for a particular product.

3.6

Use discounts and warranty wisely

Discounts are much more than just cutting prices to shift slow moving or old stock. They are also a promotional tool that you use to encourage people to buy now rather than later, or to buy more.

■ **Introductory discount.** Use a discount to encourage new customers to try you out and buy your products. This is often used by mail order and Internet businesses, which give the customer a discount on their first purchase. It's easily done, because the business will have the customer's delivery address and can easily tell if they buy again.

■ **Two for one.** Sometimes a business will package two different products for the price of one. This is simply a free sample. So, when a shopper buys their normal shampoo, they are given a face cream free of charge. Hopefully, they will like it, and buy the face cream next time.

one minute wonder Is there another company that has a complimentary product to yours that you could package together? You could jointly offer the package at a discount. It works in both business to business and consumer markets.

■ Loyalty points. You could reward existing customers for their loyalty. These schemes use a system to give free gifts according to how many points the customer collects. The Air Miles reward programme is a classic loyalty scheme, as is the Holiday Inn Priority Club. Some credit card companies now offer similar schemes, with cash back or discounts according to how much money is spent each month.

■ Time-limited discount. These schemes force people to buy now rather than later. The end-of-season sale is the classic example, as are time-stamped vouchers or coupons. The salesperson saying, "I can get you 10% off this if you buy today" is another variation of the theme.

■ Sell-up schemes. The sell-up tactic encourages the customer to spend more money. Three-for-the-price-of-two is a modern version of the 20% off if you spend more than $50.

While all these schemes help you make more sales, they do affect your profit margin. So, before you go ahead, you must estimate the additional sales and the impact on your profits.

Mail order and Internet businesses always offer a no-quibble money-back guarantee, as it eliminates the risk to customers. They will always have returns and have to carry the cost of delivery. However, they can resell the product to a business that specializes in selling returns.

You must also think about the impact of your statutory warranty and any money-back guarantee. No product is 100% perfect, and you will always have some failures. It's often cheaper and better for your reputation to replace an unsatisfactory product without question, rather than try to repair it. But any cost will hit your bottom line.

Discounts are a great way to encourage people to try your product and to stay with you, but use them sparingly.

Look at added-value and value-added

Many people get confused by the difference between added-value and value-added. Both are about how you increase the value of your products, but they operate in different ways.

We use the word value rather than price because it's all about what the customer thinks. The simple way to understand this is to remember that price is what the customer pays and value is what they think something's worth.

■ **Added-value.** This increases the perceived value. You can usually increase the value of your product at minimal cost through better packaging or minor add-ons. Your objective is to make the customer feel that the product has more value.

■ **Value-added.** This term is used when the actual value and price are both increased. You, or a third party, adds something else to your product that actually increases its price and, therefore, its value.

Added-value is not about increasing price; it's more about creating a competitive advantage. For example, Emirates Airways increased the perceived value of its flights when it added personal stereo

> **"**Amazon's value-added is not about its delivery, but about its computer technology. It knows more about the personal tastes of 20 or 30 million customers than the local shop used to know about just a few**"** **Andrew Grove, former CEO of Intel**

sockets and TVs in every seat. It was the only airline where passengers could watch and listen to whatever they wanted. Similarly, Hyundai was the first manufacturer to give a five year warranty. Both businesses increased the perceived value of their products.

In the case of value-added, on the other hand, it's usually another company that adds something to your product to sell it as something else. Industry does this a lot. For example, a company that makes generators will take a sub-unit, such as an engine, and add it to other sub-units to create an automated motor generator set. Companies that manufacture medical devices for hospitals do exactly the same with computers, printers and sensors.

In some industries, such as book publishing, there are people who just do this for a living. They're known as packagers. They think of a concept and sell it to a publisher. Then they find a writer, an illustrator and a cover designer who will create the book under their guidance. In effect, they have value-added different skills to each of the other participants.

You need to keep your eyes open for simple things that you can add to your products to create added-value. And you need to watch out for other businesses that have the potential to take your products and create another value-added product.

Added-value and value-added are easy ways to make your product stand out from those of your competitors.

3.8

Create great packaging and design

People make so many judgements based on how your product looks. It can look cheap and nasty or an expensive product. The actual shape, colour and design can make it look sexy, modern or old-fashioned. Perfume manufacturers know this better than anyone. They spend more on the bottle and the packaging than they do to make the fragrance itself.

If you sell in a shop, the position where your product sits on the shelf and what your packaging looks like is incredibly important. Both of these factors tell the potential buyer about the quality of your product and what sort of company you are.

If you sell off the Internet or by mail order, it's the look of your website or catalogue that's important. The quality of the paper and the standard of your photographs send a message to the buyer. We call these your tangibles. If you sell a service, your tangibles are the way you answer the phone, how quickly you reply to queries and what your premises and your brochures look like.

Let's assume that you ask three builders to come round to your house to look at some potential work. Which one would you choose if

one minute wonder Take photos of your premises and products. Show them to your friends and ask what they think about the company. Get a friend to phone your business with a simple question about something like prices. Then ask what they thought about how the query was handled.

the first arrived in a rusty old van, the second in a clean and smart pick-up truck and the third in a Porsche? Most people would opt for the one in the business-like pick-up truck.

■ **Support your brand values.** Whilst it's good to make your product, your packaging and your tangibles look different to those of your competitors, it is essential to make them support your brand values.
■ **Don't turn off prospective customers.** When people see your product for the first time, they are usually in the preference stage. Make sure there is no reason to delete you from their options.

The colour of your packaging also tells the buyer about you. Although there are some cultural differences, blue often implies wisdom, reassurance and stability; red energy, passion and power; purple wisdom, royalty and sophistication; and brown simplicity, comfort and endurance.
The style of the language you use in your promotional material, letters and emails also says a lot about you. If you use confusing language, with long words and complicated sentences, it will look as if you are hiding something. It might even give the impression that you are sneaky and dishonest.

People judge the quality of your product by its packaging and the way you and your premises look.

3.9

Badge to reach new markets

Some businesses expand into new markets by appearing to create new products. In reality, all they've done is bundle or unbundle an existing product in order to sell it under a new brand. Or they have purchased someone else's product and badged it as their own.

A classic example of this approach was Thorn-EMI in the 1960s and 70s. It was the largest manufacturer of televisions in the UK and in the top ten in the world. It also owned half a dozen chains of shops on the British high street under different brands. The company encouraged the shops to compete, and sold the same televisions in different packaging as Radio Rentals, Reddifusion, Ferguson, Decca and HMV.

Similarly, pet food companies and tool manufacturers such as Black & Decker do the same. They manufacture two or three similar product ranges, and often market them under different brands. One is aimed at consumers, the other at professional users such as builders, in the case of Black & Decker, and animal breeders, in the case of pet foods. They have taken this approach because the original brand has an image and reputation that doesn't fit in the professional market.

In the computer industry, companies such as Dell purchase off-the-shelf monitors from a Chinese manufacturer and badge or brand them as their own product. Often the same monitor will be badged by many other computer companies. It's only the original manufacturer's label on the rear that gives it away. Sometimes we call this OEM (Original Equipment Manufacturer).

In Europe, many of the large food retailers get manufacturers to produce certain foods and drinks as the shop's own brand products. These are usually lower quality than the original product and placed in low-cost packaging to position them as cheaper alternatives. They are known as 'own label' products. Nowadays, they are a major element of the retailer's overall profits.

Consider this approach for your business. See if you can find another product that doesn't compete too directly with your own, then think about either badging it as your own or creating a new brand in a new market area.

Many successful businesses create different products and re-brand them to compete with each other to increase overall sales.

Look where people buy

Place is the third of the four 'P's in marketing – it's where customers go to buy your products. The traditional boundaries have been broken down, and these days place can mean far more than shops and salespeople. Many opportunities have opened up in terms of place, and, using the Internet, you can now sell to anyone in the world. It sounds simple, but it isn't. Getting your product in front of a potential customer is a complex issue.

Think beyond bricks and mortar

In the last century, you usually bought a consumer product from a shop or a mail order catalogue. In the same way, businesses either bought from sales-people or trade merchants. Nowadays, however, there are no rules for where and from whom you buy.

When selling a product, you must use as many sales outlets as possible, so that it's easy for the customer to buy from you.

■ **Mail order.** This can be successful for both business and consumer markets. These days, customers either send an order by post, call an order-line or place an order on the Internet.

■ **Catalogues.** People deliver catalogues to homes and businesses for all types of product areas. The customer orders by phone, the Internet or from an agent who calls a few days later to collect the catalogue.

■ **Off the page advertising.** This is a specialist area of advertising, with one or two products in a single advertisement. The customer orders by post or calls an order line.

■ **Sales agents.** These are self-employed people who call at shops to sell a handful of products. You pay them a commission each time they sell one of your products and deliver it direct to the customer.

"I am the world's worst salesman, therefore, I must make it easy for people to buy"

F.W. Woolworth, founder of Woolworth's

■ **Van sales.** This refers to salespeople in a van. They call at homes and businesses to sell things such as food, cleaning chemicals, tools and parts for vehicle repairs.

■ **Theme fairs.** Many product areas have specialist fairs, such as food festivals and wedding fairs. At such a fair, you can hire a stand and display your products just as you would in a shop.

■ **Buying groups.** This is a number of businesses that group together to bulk purchase items such as office stationery at a discount. They can operate over the Internet.

■ **Internet shops.** Companies such as Amazon sell solely over the Internet; others use an Internet shop to extend their geographic reach.

■ **Mobile phones.** In some parts of Europe and the Far East you can buy rail and bus tickets and car parking through your mobile phone.

■ **Auction Internet sites.** There are many people who work from home and run eBay shops that have sales over $500,000 per annum.

While this is not an exhaustive list, it does show that there are many ways that you can reach your prospective customers, whether they are businesses or consumers. You're limited only by your imagination.

There are many ways to reach customers, so don't just limit yourself to one, two or even three places.

4.2

Identify where your customers will go

At the end of the day, there is no point in having the best product in the world if customers cannot get hold of it. So, you must think about where they will buy it. Ask yourself, do they need to buy it locally, because they want to touch and see it before they decide? Or will they be happy to buy it on the Internet from another country?

In Secret 4.1, we looked at some of the places where people might buy from you. But, at the end of the day, it's about their preference and convenience. Imagine that you produce security products for the home – padlocks, bolts and door locks. Where will your customers expect to buy your products? In a small independent shop, a national DIY chain, from a security company, through a mail order catalogue or via the Internet. The answer is probably all of them.

What you must do is ask your customers what they would prefer. And a survey is one of the best ways to do this. If you structure it carefully, you will get two sorts of information.

"No great marketing decisions have ever been made on just quantitative data"

John Scully, American business guru

■ **Quantitative data.** These are the facts – the numbers of people who answered yes or no to a particular question. So, for example, you can find out what percentage of people would prefer to buy on the Internet.

■ **Qualitative data.** These are thoughts, feelings and comments. The answers to these questions tell you why the customer made the decisions they did. So, for example, the qualitative data will give you reasons why they would prefer to buy on the Internet.

The problems arise when you rely only on quantitative data. So, for example, a customer might buy on the Internet, but only after having seen your product in a shop. You will get that information only from a face-to-face survey rather than form filling.

Whenever you do a survey, you must conduct it in two halves. Firstly, ask the yes/no questions to get the quantitative data. Analyse it, and decide what information from the results you need to clarify. Then you must do a series of telephone or face-to-face interviews to get the qualitative data. You then have the complete picture, and can make a judgement on what you should do.

You must discover where your customers would prefer to buy from, but that's often easier said than done.

4.3

Multiple channels will get you in

Many people think that, if you create a good product, every shop will clamour to sell it. Nothing's further from the truth. They've usually got enough products on their shelves already, and will be reluctant to take on something new and untested.

Large shops don't like to have many suppliers and are very reluctant to add a new one. So, it's often better to approach an existing supplier who'd be willing to add your product to their range. But, of course, they will want a percentage.

Small independent shops are difficult to supply unless you have people who can regularly visit each one. Some companies do it with a team of merchandisers, who re-stock the shop every week or so. But most sell to a wholesaler or distributor that supplies the local shops.

Specialist shops buy from sales agents or at trade fairs. Agents specialize in a particular type of product, such as gifts. You will find it hard to find a good agent who is willing to take your product on top of the half dozen they already have. They will want exclusive rights in an area or territory, and you will have to give the shop a display stand to show off your product in the best light.

"Channels can be viewed as sets of independent organizations involved in making a product or service available to the consumer"

Louis Stern, American investment banker

If you want to succeed, you must have a mix of different sales outlets and methods. Marketing people call these channels, and everyone in the chain will want a percentage of your sales. You'll have to do some work too.

■ **Push your products through the channel.** You must continuously promote your product to the distributor or the agent. Don't forget that they have more than just your product to sell.

■ **Pull your product through the channel.** You must promote your products to potential customers, and tell them which distributors and outlets stock them.

■ **Manage channel members.** You must agree a level of sales and monitor it. Give incentives to get the salespeople to sell more at certain times of the year, and tell them when you plan to run an advertising campaign to promote your product.

The business market is similar, except companies tend to mix direct salespeople, catalogues and retail outlets.

You must identify, manage and monitor the chain of people and companies that will get your product into the hands of the consumer.

4.4

Use silent salesmen

Mail order is a very good way to sell to customers that you wouldn't normally be able to reach. Nowadays, this approach is used in both the consumer and business markets, though in the latter it is usually called a sales catalogue rather than mail order. This is also a great way to tell your customers about special offers and new products.

If you have enough products of your own, you can create your own mail-order catalogue. But that is rare and something that needs specialist skills. There are many advertising companies that will create a product database and design you a mail-order catalogue. You will need the database to manage prices and reduce costs when you create the next version of your catalogue, which is at least every quarter.

Most businesses convince a mail-order company to carry their product, just as a shop does. In many ways, it's like advertising. You will have to supply photographs and pay to be in a good position in their

case study Operating a mail-order or catalogue business is very specialized and requires a lot of time and effort. For example, Lakeland Stores in the UK has a catalogue for each product group – kitchen, cleaning, gifts and so

"Every word, sentence, and photograph in your catalogue should have one specific purpose, to lead your potential customer to the order page" **Anon**

catalogue. Many mail-order companies don't actually stock products, but pass the orders on to the companies making the products, so they can drop-ship them directly to the customer.

In some European countries, companies use part-time agents to deliver and collect catalogues to and from homes and small businesses. These agents also handle the orders and deliver the products to the customers a week or so later. They are paid a small commission on all sales that they make.

Some industrial companies use small catalogues to supplement their direct sales force. You can do the same with a single sheet of paper – or you might want to fold it in half to create four pages. Your sales-person can leave it with the customer, who can order by phone, fax or on the Internet.

You can also send cheap post cards to your existing customers to get them to buy products on special offer. Just make sure that you tell your channel members what you are doing.

Mail order and catalogue sales are a specialized area, but you can easily do a cut-down version yourself.

on. It regularly creates new versions of these with special offers so that a customer receives a new catalogue every few weeks. Unless you're already experienced in mail order, it's not worth doing it yourself.

4.5

Add affiliate schemes

Affiliate selling is a term coined by Internet companies. However, the concept has been around for some time in a slightly different form. It was called sales commission or revenue sharing. The idea is to pay a third party every time they introduce a customer to your business.

With an affiliate scheme, the third party doesn't actually sell your products, it just promotes your business and refers potential customers to you. In many ways, it's like advertising. You can either pay the other party a small amount for each enquiry (known as commission per lead) or every time you make a sale because of their referral (known as commission per sale).

■ **Membership groups.** Chambers of Commerce, golf clubs and frequent flyer schemes always need to add value to their membership. One way that they can do this is to offer their members a discount off

case study A small household insurance company in the UK donates £1 to a charity for blind people every time a consumer requests a quote on the Internet or

of a particular product. In effect, the company that makes the product is paying a nominal commission to the group's organization in such a deal, but no money actually changes hands.

■ **Other businesses.** Think about other businesses that sell a different sort of product into your target customer group. You could convince them to place some information about your products on their website with a click-through. Or, you could run a joint promotional campaign whereby you offer both products as a package and at a discount. You can use leaflets or advertising as the promotional tool.

■ **Your suppliers.** The suppliers you use have their own customer base. So why not treat them like a membership group, and offer them a discount off of your products. Alternatively, suggest that you do a joint promotion to each other's customers.

■ **The charity sector.** Charities and good causes can add an ethical element to your product. If there is a choice between two similar products, something like 85% of people will choose the one that supports a charity. Children's charities are the most popular. In order to promote your product in conjunction with a particular charity, you need to donate money for every product you sell or enquiry you receive.

Marketing is about opportunities. You must open your mind and grab any chance to contact potential customers. Affiliate schemes, or revenue sharing, is one of them. (See also Secret 6.7)

Marketing is about innovation and you must explore every method to reach potential customers.

through one of its agents. Since the company started to promote this scheme, it has seen a 15% increase in quotations and an 8% increase in sales.

Devise your promotional mix

Promotion is the fourth and final marketing 'P' and is the sexy side of the business. There are hundreds of ways that you can promote your business and products, and you need to create your own promotional mix. A variety of strategies must be used, and what you have to do is choose the method that's right for customers at each stage in the buying process. You'll need to devise, manage and monitor many different promotional activities.

5.1

"Shoot with a rifle, not a shotgun"

Nobody can afford to promote their product to everyone. You just don't have enough money for that. And anyway, bear in mind that most people will probably never buy your product and many won't want to buy it at the moment.

The key to promotion is to use your money wisely. The rule is "shoot with a rifle, not a shotgun". Ask yourself three questions.

1 What do my potential customers read, watch or listen to? To find out, you'll have to ask them. Or, you can search through various media directories and look at their target readership.

2 What other products do my potential customers buy? The point here is to find out where to target your advertising. If you sell luxury cars, for example, you might put your adverts in a golfing publication or posters at a golf club.

3 How will I recognize when they're ready to buy? This is more difficult, but you must remember that you can't use the same promotional material at all the buying stages (See Secret 2.3).

"Half the money I spend on advertising is wasted; the problem is I do not know which half"

Lord Leverhulme, British industrialist of the early 20th century

During the first stage of the customers buying process, you must make sure that they know about you. Use awareness advertising and entries in directories such as Yellow Pages. But remember that, unless you sell your product all over the country, you will waste money advertising in all the national newspapers. In fact, each newspaper and magazine targets a particular type of reader, and you must match this with the work you did on your ideal customer (Secret 2.2).

Even if you stand in the street and hand leaflets to people who pass by, you must be selective. Go back to the demographics of your ideal customer, and only give leaflets to people who look the right age.

In Secret 2.4, we looked at how many people can get involved in a purchase, and how they want different sorts of information. Technical people don't need or want your corporate brochure. And often, the person who actually has the money doesn't want the technical specification of your product.

Similarly, if you do a mail shot, check that the companies or the people you are targeting are currently at their address and haven't moved. And, if you address them by name, check that you have used the correct spelling. Few things upset potential customers more than getting their names wrong.

Don't throw money away by promoting products to everybody; focus your efforts on people who are ready to buy.

5.2

Grab their attention

Every piece of promotion is about communication. You tell your market audience something about your business, your products and what you stand for. And you expect them to do something as a result. But nowadays, people always seem to be in a rush. Their time is limited and they'll quickly move on if you don't grab their attention and keep their interest in what you're saying.

Marketing people use a check list, known as AIDA, to help them with any piece of communication they create. It doesn't matter whether it's a letter, an email, an advert, a brochure or a radio commercial. The same rules apply.

■ **A = Attention.** You are probably interrupting your target audience, so you must grab their attention and make them listen to what you're saying. It could be a headline, a photograph or a jingle.

■ **I = Interest.** When you've grabbed their attention you need to draw them in. You must say things that will interest them and keep them fixed on what you're saying.

one minute wonder Take one of your brochures and ask yourself, does the cover make me want to open it and read the contents? If it doesn't, you've broken the first two rules – that you must grab the people's attention and keep their interest.

■ **D = Desire.** This is the most difficult part. But you must create and build their desire for your offering, your product and your business. Think about the expression "sell the sizzle, not the sausage".

■ **A = Action.** You will have a reason to talk to them and they need to know what you want them to do. Otherwise it's "so what" for them and a waste of money for you. Do you want them to remember your slogan, look at your website, phone you or go and buy your product?

It doesn't really matter how carefully you've written your piece of promotion, or how wonderful you think it is. What really matters is what your target audience think, and whether they will do what you want. You must try out your promotional piece with some of your target audience and measure the result. Do a small sample and see what happens; make a couple of changes, and do it again. The marketing mantra with promotion is, "test, test and test".

Promotion is about communication. The most important things are what you say, how you say it and what you expect your potential customers to do.

Cover all bases

Promotion is not about advertising and brochures alone, and we have loads of tools at our fingertips to bring into play. Indeed, you must be prepared to use every tool at your disposal to create the right mix of promotional work to handle potential customers in any given situation.

To begin with, all you need to do is pick one or two of the promotional tools in your armoury. Just make sure that they fit into the right stage of the buying process.

1 **Need or want stage.** You must make your target audience aware of your brand and what your company does. Use awareness advertising, posters, mail shots, directories, search engine positioning, competitions, give-aways, sponsorship and news releases. Keep repeating your message as people easily forget.

2 **Knowledge stage.** Here, you must give enough information to enable your potential customers to make informed decisions. Use advertising, brochures, newsletters, press releases, feature articles, facts sheets, trade shows and exhibitions, seminars, your website and your blog.

"What really decides consumers to buy or not to buy is the content of your advertising, not its form" David Ogilvy, advertising guru

Preference stage. At this point, you want your audience to choose your product over one of your competitors'. Use corporate brochures, trade shows and exhibitions, testimonials, case studies, money-back guarantees, free trials or other pilot schemes to reduce the risk for them.

Buy and justify stage. This point is all about getting the customers to buy now. So, use time-limited discounts, low-interest loans and money-off vouchers to encourage them not to delay their decision for too long.

Your purpose at each stage is to give the customer just enough information to move onto the next point. In the final stage, you only have one aim: that is, to make them go and buy your product now.

Don't forget that advertising can take two forms. Awareness advertising is all about getting your brand into the mind of the customer. But in the knowledge stage you must use more detailed advertising to give them quite a bit of information about your product and your business.

You must pick the right mix of promotional tools for each stage in the buying process to move potential customers to the next stage.

5.4

Design posters and advertising

Most advertising is about how you build awareness of your business and your products. Your objective is either to make people remember you, or to make them want to know more. The exception is an advertisement to actually sell your product through the mail. Then you are "selling off the page".

You can advertise in lots of different media, including the press, TV and radio. You can use posters, postcards, leaflet drops, letters and banner adverts on websites. Unfortunately, people nowadays are bombarded with advertising – it is estimated that, on average, Americans see over 300 adverts every day, for example. Given this deluge of information and messages, you must create something that's really memorable if you want to stand out from the crowd.

A slogan is one of the best ways to do this, especially if you are using posters, where you often have less than a second to grab the public's attention. The best slogans either come from a 'eureka' moment or from a brain-storming session with your colleagues.

"Make it simple. Make it memorable. Make it inviting to look at. Make it fun to read"

Leo Burnett, advertising executive

■ **Make it striking.** Have something that sets you apart from the competition and sticks in people's minds. Think, 'Just do it', from Nike and 'Vorsprung durch Technik', from Audi.

■ **Make it unforgettable.** A good way to make people remember is to give your slogan a rhythm. Similarly, you could make it a rhyme. Think 'Beanz Meanz Heinz' and Mazda's 'Zoom zoom'.

■ **Make it say what you do.** Try to make the slogan state a benefit, so that it 'says what it does on the tin'. Examples include 'We try harder', from Avis and 'The ultimate driving machine', from BMW.

■ **Make it unusual.** It doesn't have to be words. It can be a sound, shape or a picture. Most people know the shape of the Coca Cola bottle and the sound of the Nokia tune, whether they have these products or not.

■ **Make it emotional.** You must make people feel happy and warm, not sad and cold. Think of the adverts for Jack Daniel's Tennessee whiskey and 'Finger lickin' good', from KFC.

■ **Make it everywhere.** You must put your slogan on every piece of communication. On the sign outside your building, at the foot of every letter and email you send, and on your product packaging.

You want people to remember your name. So associate your name with a memorable slogan or saying. Then they will remember you.

Use a a memorable slogan or strap line to stand out from the crowd and make people remember you.

5.5

Use the press and media

One of the best uses of the press, radio and television is in educating your market about your business and the benefits of your products. This is particularly true if you sell pure services, such as accountancy, legal advice, training or consultancy.

After all, most people believe what's written in the press. And so it follows that articles in the press serve to dramatically increase your credibility and your status. What's more, they'll help you build a relationship with your potential customers that doesn't cost lots of money. The downside to using such media is that it's almost impossible to control the press.

Press releases and feature articles are a wonderful way to inform potential customers while they are in the knowledge stage of the buying process. Many people tear articles out of newspapers and keep them. A press release should be one or two pages in length, and it must always be dated and double-spaced. It has to be newsworthy as well; if it isn't, you'll need to create some news. A classic way to generate a newsworthy angle is to do a survey about what people think about something, then issue the results as a press release.

■ **Lead paragraph.** The first paragraph of the press release must cover the complete story in just 50 to 100 words. Most people are lazy, and journalists are no different. So, keep the opener to the minimum amount of text you'd like to see in print.

■ **Detail paragraph.** This is more detail about the story. It should cover each of the five 'W's in depth: "Who, what, when, why and where."

■ **Quote paragraph.** Here, you put a quote from the owner of your business or someone else you've already mentioned in the story.

■ **More information.** This is just what it says – more about the story. Therefore, it should not be just background information on your business or your products.

■ **Note to editors.** The last paragraph is where you should explain more about your company, its history and its products. Here, you should also put contact details, including your name, business address and phone number.

If you have an idea for a feature article, you should write a brief synopsis, and phone the editor to sell them the idea. They will ask for an outline, so send them your synopsis. Choose the newspaper or magazine carefully, as they will want exclusive publication rights.

Use the press to publish articles about your products and business so you can educate your potential customers.

5.6

Create press releases and drip feeds

It's all very well for you to spend lots of money on advertising campaigns to create awareness, but you must also keep your brand at the front of people's minds. They have very short memories, and research tells us that they will only instantly recall two or three brand names for each type of product.

How many brands of trainers can you instantly think of? Probably two, most likely Nike and Adidas. But Puma was the first on the market, and the brand is still very big. Since you don't have a limitless budget, you need to be imaginative in ways to drip feed your brand into the minds of your target customers.

one minute wonder Spend time with a monthly planner and devise a schedule of drip feed promotions over the next year. You must do something at least every month.

■ **News alerts for the media.** Nowadays we live in a sound-bite society, and the media are always looking for little stories to fill the gaps. Put out a one- or two-paragraph news alert on things such as latest orders, a new member of staff or a new promotional campaign.

■ **Expert comment in the media.** Use some of the web techniques described in Secret 6.1 to build a platform for your business. Journalists and news programmes are always searching for quotes from experts, as they will add credibility to their stories.

■ **Drip feed advertising.** Produce short versions of your awareness advertising and run them in bursts. For example, take the slogan from your radio campaign and put it in the press as a series of small adverts.

■ **Newsletters.** You can print these and mail them out or produce them as emails. If you print them, you should do one every three months. If you email them, you should make them shorter and more frequent – once a month is good.

■ **Giveaways and promotional gifts.** These are token gifts for your customers and prospective customers. Create something interesting with your logo that they will keep. Things like pens, key rings, coffee mugs and mouse mats work well.

Whatever you decide to do, you must make it look as though it's part of your overall campaign. This is all about adding more and more, to drip feed your brand into your market.

You must find ways to keep your brand at the front of your potential customer's minds because people have very short memories.

5.7

Connect to buyers at trade events

The people who visit exhibitions and trade shows and fairs are usually in the knowledge or preference stages of the buying process (see Secret 2.3). In other words, they are almost ready to buy. So these are ideal places to promote your business and your products to an almost captive audience.

The problem with any form of exhibition or show is that you must plan them well in advance if you want to get them right. The last minute panic approach just does not work. So, here are the guiding points to enable you to have a successful trade fair.

■ **Decide the best approach.** Pick the trade show that is best for your business and decide what you want to get out of it. Agree the image that you want to convey to the audience and be crystal clear about what you want them to remember.

■ **Book the space.** Twelve to nine months before the show is due to take place, look at what space is available. You should pick a spot on a corner, near a food area or opposite a major company. Book it, sign the contract and pay the deposit.

one minute wonder Take a minute to plan a short workshop for a week before the show. This will be for all the people who'll be on your stand, and will be your chance to tell them what to do and how to behave.

■ **Devise a theme.** Six months before the show, you must devise a theme for your stand that is topical and in keeping with your brand. Choose a designer, and think about how you're going to publicize the fact that you'll be at the show.

■ **Develop promotional material.** Submit your entry to the show catalogue three months ahead of the show. Book any hotels that you might need and order promotional gifts, leaflets and brochures.

■ **Press packs and releases.** One month before, update your website and prepare a press pack in a folder, with leaflets and a backgrounder. Issue a press release and send free tickets to all your major customers and the movers and shakers in your industry.

A good way to get ideas for your stand is to go to another show and take a camera. Look carefully at the stands. Which look welcoming? Can you read their message in one second from ten metres? Learn from what you see and adapt the ideas to your stand.

Shows and exhibitions are great places to promote your business and products to people who are almost ready to buy.

5.8

Network with movers and shakers

Networking is a great way to influence the movers and shakers in your local area or industry. These are the people who have influence and can recommend your business to others. Organized events are the best, because you can meet people and arrange to spend an hour or two together to get to know each other.

There are many places where you can network. The obvious ones are chambers of commerce and trade associations. But there are also conferences, exhibitions, training courses and seminars. In fact, you can network wherever you are – you never know who you might meet at a railway station or airport.

Before you go to a networking event, you must get yourself prepared. Make sure that you have a pen, some paper and plenty of business cards. Dress appropriately for the event – it's nice if you can stand out a bit, without looking weird. When you arrive, tell yourself that you are there to network, not to drink coffee and talk to the people you already know. Plan to spend between five and eight minutes with each new person you meet.

one minute wonder Look at your own business card. Does it clearly explain what your business does and what it stands for? If not, then get some printed with your proposition on the back.

■ **Approach people.** Don't be afraid to talk to anyone, whether they're on their own or in a small group. Just go up to them, say hello and introduce yourself.

■ **Engage with them.** You must be interested in the people you meet and want to know what they do. At the same time, you must come across as an interesting person. Ask them questions about their business and tell them a bit about yourself.

■ **Exchange business cards.** Ask for their card first, look at it for a few seconds and then give them one of your cards. If you feel that you'd like to talk to them further, suggest that you meet another time.

■ **Sort and decide.** When you get back to your office, look at each card and decide with whom you'd like to develop a relationship. Split the cards into three piles – one for yes, one for maybe and the last for no.

■ **Follow up.** Email each of the people in the yes pile with some dates for a meeting. Then send emails to the people in the maybe pile saying that you enjoyed meeting them and hope to see them again.

Look friendly and confident when networking, but don't hand out business cards or leaflets like confetti.

5.9

Use loyalty schemes

Even if you don't expect your customers to buy from you again – for instance, if you are a house builder – you must do everything to make them happy. After all, you want them to recommend you to other potential clients, not to slate you. Satisfied customers become loyal, and they can support your business by telling their friends about you.

Of course, the quality of your product is important, but it's your brand values and your service that makes customers loyal to you and your brand. If you ask any business what they think of their account-ant, you'll get one of three answers. They'll say that they are great, okay or that they're bad. Even if they're terrible, though, the customer will often stay with them, simply because they're too lazy to change account-ant. If another accountancy firm sells to them, however, they are likely to move like a shot.

You must aim to be in a position where all your customers will answer 'great' to the question of how good is your service.

"Loving your customer boils down to one thing – creating an almost fanatical sense of loyalty"

Brad Antin

■ **Monitor how many customers you lose.** This is called churn. Ask your customers how you are doing. Send them a customer satisfaction survey, and phone them as soon as possible after the sale to ask them what they think.

■ **Create a loyalty scheme.** Award customers with points every time they buy something. Create a scheme such as Air Miles, and let them choose between shopping vouchers from various high street shops. Most stores do these.

■ **Keep them informed.** Start a monthly or quarterly newsletter to tell your customers what you are doing. Give it a human face by talking about what some of your staff do when they're not at work.

■ **Engage with them.** Create a forum on your website or start a blog. We cover these in Secrets 6.5 and 6.4, respectively.

These days, people like to be proud that they've bought your products. Loyalty schemes are just one weapon in your armoury to make customers feel good. Use them to reinforce your brand values.

You must build a sense of loyalty into your customers, so they support you and recommend you to others.

5.10

Always support your brand

History tells us that your brand is the most important thing in your business. And that's true if you sell to other businesses or to consumers. Strong brands are easily recognized by potential customers, and some have become household names in their own right – Xerox, Hoover and Google, to name just a few. Others, like Rolex and Porsche, tell everyone about your status in society.

Whatever values you create for your brand, you must make sure that everything supports them. Ask yourself these questions.

1 **Does your logo support your brand values?** The Shell logo is recognized all round the world, and its yellow and red signify energy and power.

2 **Is your typeface old-fashioned?** The size and shape of the font that you use in your literature and on your website must reinforce your brand values.

"Products, like people, have person- alities, which can make or break them in the market place"

David Ogilvy, advertising guru

What does your tone and style say about you? The way you write says so much about your values. For example, if your words are complicated and long-winded, you'll look sneaky.

Does your packaging support your brand? The packaging is the first thing people see about your product. It's the envelope, if you post it, and the box, if it sits on a shelf.

5 **What about your other tangibles?** Your premises, vehicles and the way your staff dress tell your customers what you're like as a business. Make sure they look as though they support your values.

6 **How about your day to day communications?** The way you answer the phone, as well as your letters and emails, also tell people what you're like as a company.

Strong brands have clear values that people understand and can relate to. Volvo stands for safety, for example, and Audi for technology. These brands have functional appeal. Others, like Apple, have emotional appeal. If you can create emotional appeal for your customers, they will become passionate about you and buy everything you sell.

McDonald's ensures that everything they do supports their image, and so they are recognized globally.

Get on the Internet

The Internet has opened up many opportunities for businesses to create new products and find new ways to market them. And a one-man business can now compete on almost equal terms with a multinational. Today, there are numerous freelancers and small companies that specialize in marketing solely on the Internet. You don't need to be an expert, but you must be inquisitive, have an open mind and understand what it could do for your business.

6.1

Make yourself visible

Ten years ago, people found out about companies and products from newspapers, magazines, exhibitions and word of mouth. The Internet has changed that. Nowadays, it's the first place they go.

People will search for your type of product every hour of the day. And they will check up on your company through your website seven days a week. Even if they don't know the address of your website, they should be able to find you through the popular search engines.

Most people won't look beyond the first ten results, and you should appear in the top five, if you can. You must get specialist advice from an SEO expert (Search Engine Optimization), as well as doing some of the basic things yourself.

■ **The right design.** It's all very well having a great looking website, but what matters most is how it functions. Check that your site has been designed with SEO in mind. You must have things such as headings, meta-tags and image tags. Go to www.websitegrader.com to see the marketing effectiveness of your site. It's free.

■ **The right keywords.** Research the words that people use most when looking for your type of product. You may be able to do this yourself. Alternatively, use a site such as www.wordtracker.com, which provides a free, although limited, service.

■ **The right links.** Talk to your suppliers and other people you work with to exchange links to each other's websites. Google, in particular, likes lots of links into your site from other people's.

■ **The right content.** All the search engines rank sites according to how much content they have and how often it changes. One of the easiest ways to add content is to embed a blog into your site using free software from www.wordpress.com.

■ **The right places.** Add your business to the main web directories. Many offer free entries, and you should at least be in DMOZ (www.dmoz.org) and the Yahoo Directory (http://dir.yahoo.com). Both are free and have good links with Google.

The Internet has almost totally replaced trade directories and Yellow Pages as the primary place where people look for products and services. If they can't find you in the top ten search results, then you almost don't exist. So you must spend time, effort and a bit of money to make sure you are there.

Nowadays people are in control and use the Internet to find the products that they want. If they don't find you, you don't exist.

6.2

Be a shop window

Your website is the first place people go to find out about your products and your business. The second is friends, who they may ask for advice and recommendations. Think of your website as your store front or shop window, the purpose of which is to entice customers to come inside and browse.

Like any promotional tool, you must design your website for your specific target market. If you have two or three totally different markets, you might need two or three different websites. It's not just about the look and feel of your site; it's also the technology that you use.

■ **Think about speed.** Your first page must load quickly, so it's not good to have lots of flash or large images on your home page. If I had a dollar for every time someone pressed 'skip intro', I'd be a very wealthy man. Don't assume that every user has a fast connection to the Internet.
■ **Echo your brand values.** You must also make sure that the feel of your website reinforces your brand values. Have a look at www.apple.com and www.nike.com. You'll see that their websites look exactly like their shops, their adverts and their brochures.

one minute wonder Ask your web designer to embed a blog on your site. You'll then be able to add information and news very quickly to maintain interest in your site – and at almost no cost.

■ **Make clear statements.** Ensure that the home page on your website says clearly what you do in the first few lines. Rewrite your proposition (see Secret 2.6) so it's short and snappy and put it in a bold font.

■ **Add a human side.** These days, it's possible to find a product, check it out and buy it without any human contact at all. You must add a human side to your website by having pictures of people – preferably real people, who work in your business. Add names and contact details so that customers will feel reassured by a smiling face.

■ **Keep it current.** In some ways, your website has replaced your corporate brochure. But it's got much more potential than that. It's so easy to update and add things that you must change it in some way every month. And the search engines love you when you do that.

These days, the website has almost totally replaced the company brochure. But make sure that it's a living thing, just like a shop window. Don't let it get old, tired and dusty. You must thoroughly revamp it at least every two years.

Think about your target customers and your brand values before you design your website. Everything must fit together.

Write email newsletters

Email newsletters are the modern version of the quarterly news bulletin that companies printed and posted to their customers. Printed material is great for the home, where it will often sit around before it gets read, and sometimes hangs around for days or weeks afterwards. But they are expensive to produce.

Most companies can afford to produce printed material only a few times a year. The alternative is the email newsletter which, although it might be professionally designed and written, doesn't actually cost anything to print and distribute. The downside is that it can easily be deleted before it's read, and it doesn't hang around for other people to read. Also, most countries have legislation to reduce unwanted emails, so you must ask users to sign up first.

case study There is a small US-based sales training company that sends out a weekly newsletter complete with sales tips and advice. Every email contains an advert, and, at the bottom of the

There are two different ways of producing a newsletter. The first is to send the same newsletter to everyone at the same time. Paid-for services like www.constantcontact.com and www.topica.com are a very effective way to do this. There are also free services from Google (http://groups.google.com) and Yahoo (http://groups.yahoo.com). But these let you send only plain text emails.

The second way is to automatically send every new subscriber the same sequence of newsletters from the time they sign up. Companies like www.aweber.com provide a service to do this.

Whatever way you choose you must...

1 Prepare a 12-month schedule of topics that develop into a theme. You should aim for a newsletter every month or fortnight, not every day.

2 Split long articles or features into two or three sections or chapters and send them as a series of emails. This encourages people to read the next instalment.

3 Don't get bewitched by your own words. Write, then sleep on it and read it again the next day. Change it if you think that your reader won't be interested in what you've said.

Through email marketing you can engage with your customers and gain an idea of who's interested in what you do.

document, there is a link to their website. Despite the fact that this is only a very modestly sized company, more than 30,000 people from around the world now subscribe to the newsletter.

6.4

Build blogs and podcasts

The big downside with a newsletter is that it is outbound, so search engines don't see it. But, putting the contents of the newsletter onto your website and emailing a link to each subscriber has two advantages. Firstly, the subscriber receives an email, which reminds them about you. Secondly, search engines see the new content, which improves your ranking.

A blog or a podcast is the best and easiest way to do this. A blog is a series of web pages that are linked through a database, so you can search them to find one that covers a particular topic. Readers can also leave comments, which will give you an insight into what interests them.

■ **Create a blog.** It's very easy to create a blog with services such as www.blogger.com and www.wordpress.com. Both are free.
■ **Link it in.** You can also put a link from your website to your blog and vice versa. If you decide to exploit the modern social networking phenomenon, you can place a link to your blog in your messages in Twitter and Facebook (see Secret 6.8).

"Blogging is the next big wave of human communication. Before that it was email, and, of course, instant messaging is just real-time email"

Eric Schmidt, CEO of Google

■ **Keep it going.** It's even easier to post a new entry. The best way is to create a draft using your normal word processing software, then copy and paste it into a new post. You can easily change the look and feel to fit in with your brand values.

■ **Blog for business** In the businesses realm, blogs usually contain 'content-rich' material. Things like feature articles, how-to tutorials and case studies. Your blog readers can also subscribe through a RSS (Really Simple Syndication) or an ATOM (Atom Syndication Format) feed, so they will be told automatically when you make a new entry. You can also use Feedburner from Google (http://feedburner.google.com), which sends subscribers an automatic email with the contents of every new entry.

■ **Create a podcasts.** A podcast is either pure audio, a slide presentation or a short piece of video. You can either place it on your own website or you can use a public media server such as YouTube (www.youtube.com), Podcast Alley (www.podcastalley.com) or Apple's iTunes (www.apple.com/podcasting).

Blogs and podcasts are a way to get noticed, build your search engine ranking and engage with your customers all at once.

6.5

Offer forums and portals

The Internet has given marketing people almost unlimited opportunities to engage with the market. The pace of technology means that new ways are added almost every month. Some break new ground and become mainstream, others fall by the wayside.

■ **Web forums.** These are like noticeboards and are a wonderful way to find out what customers think of you. There are many public forums for people with a common interest, but more and more companies are creating their own, where customers can respond to the company's products. Apple has forums on the MAC, iPod and iPhone at http://discussions.apple.com, and there is a public forum for BMW enthusiasts at www.bimmerforums.com. Each site needs a moderator with the power to remove offensive posts and ban users who misuse it.

case study The forum on Sony's PlayStation website (http://boardsus.playstation.com/playstation) has company announcements and discussions between users on the pros and cons of various games and

■ **Wikis.** A Wiki is like a blog (see Secret 6.4) in which anyone can add and edit pages of information that are interlinked and indexed. The most famous Wiki is Wikipedia, the free encyclopedia with almost three million articles in English (http://wikipedia.org). You can create your own using a service such as www.wikispaces.com, and use it for people in your company to share information or for your customers to do the same. It's a useful way for your customers to share tips with others.

■ **Portals.** A web portal is a commercial website run by a third party that is dedicated to a particular interest or industry. Examples include www.weddingchannel.com in the US and www.flyingcv.com in India. Many government agencies use portals as a way into their services. A portal usually contains articles, features and news, as well as links to suppliers. Many also have a forum for users. Some portals give you a free listing, others charge a small fee or take a commission on every sale that you make through their site. It's very much like an interactive directory.

These three technologies are just some of the ways that you can engage with customers. But the Internet moves at a dramatic pace, so you must keep your eyes open for new opportunities all the time. And don't dismiss them without playing with them first, for a month or so.

In the last century a business used to interact with its customers, nowadays it has to engage with them.

products. There are millions of posts, and some topics have more than two million entries. This is a gold mine for Sony, as a source of information for discovering what their users are interested in.

6.6

Use viral marketing

Viral marketing has been around since we started to talk. But, before the rise of the Internet, it was known as word-of-mouth marketing. It's when someone tells someone else about something interesting. Businesses have now learnt to exploit this, and create messages that people are most likely to pass on.

Microsoft's free email service, Hotmail, was one of the pioneers of viral marketing on the Internet. Every email sent had an advert for Hotmail at the bottom. Now every social or business networking website uses the 'invite your friends' feature as viral marketing.

Companies like Amway and Avon rely on people to get their friends to buy the products and join the company as a distributor. This is the off-line version of viral marketing or word-of-mouth marketing.

case study To promote a new chocolate bar, Cadbury selected ten 'super agents' from thousands of applications who wanted to win a £20,000 prize. These agents had to successfully

■ Create a buzz. A company may give away new products to influential users and the media as a form of viral marketing. In 1999, TiVo produced some of the first digital video recorders, and gave them away free to web enthusiasts so that they would write about the product on their blogs and tell their friends. This is probably one of the first examples of viral marketing as we know it today.

■ Use web communities. With the advent of video sharing websites and interactive games, viral marketing has jumped to a new level. It's all about sharing an experience with your friends or joining a community. Viral marketing agencies use video clips, interactive flash games, ebooks, slide shows, SMS messages and social networking sites (see Secret 6.8).

In the UK, Cadbury's Chocolates is one of the leaders in using viral marketing. Each of it's TV adverts has over 3.5 million hits on YouTube and on its website (www.aglassandahalffullproductions.com) the company combines interactive Flash games with Twitter messages and videos placed on YouTube. In a similar way, the publisher Random House created Twitter and Facebook pages for Dan Brown's book *The Lost Symbol*. The publisher used them to share codes, puzzles, maps, and ciphers with fans. A blog was also created for the book's hero, Robert Langdon, who isn't even a real person, of course.

Viral marketing is a must for any business that sells to consumers who are under the age of 50.

complete a number of missions, film themselves and post them on the Internet. The winner was the one that got the most comments on YouTube and the most followers on Twitter.

6.7

Set up third party schemes

With the Internet, you can reach millions of potential customers either directly or through a third party. You can also make money while you sleep by earning commission from other company's products that you recommend on your own website.

If, for example, you had a recommended reading page on your website, you could place links to a bookselling site such as Amazon. And, providing you'd signed up as an Amazon Associate, you would earn a small fee every time someone bought something from Amazon via your website. The money is simply transferred into your bank account every month. Not only do you earn a bit of money, but you also improve the quality and image of your website to potential customers. This is called an affiliate scheme, but there are other kinds of schemes too, each offering different marketing possibilities.

■ **Affiliate schemes.** Internet services like www.webgains.com and www.clickbank.com provide a service where you can earn money as an affiliate or pay for leads as a merchant. In either case, you will have to be approved by the service provider and add a small piece of code to your website. In essence, this is revenue sharing or a sales commission.

"Affiliate marketing has made businesses millions and ordinary people millionaires"

Bo Bennett, entrepreneur and motivational speaker

■ **Pay-per-click services.** In some schemes, such as Google Adwords or Yahoo Sponsored Search, you pay for an action by the user rather than when you make a sale. So, when someone uses Google to search for a particular type of product, your business could appear on the top right-hand side of the page of results. You will then have to pay Google a small amount of money if the user clicks on your advert. That's why it's known as pay-per-click.

■ **Contextual advertising.** The third type of scheme is known as contextual advertising. Google is the leader with Adsense. You allow Google to place adverts on your own website that are relevant to your keywords. You get a small payment when someone clicks on one of these adverts, which you can spend on pay-per-click advertising.

All in all, affiliate schemes offer a smart way to present yourself to more potential customers through other people's websites and to open up your community of customers to other businesses through your own website.

Earn money from your website with an affiliate scheme and generate leads for your business by using the same idea from other people's websites.

6.8

Join networking sites

In the last five years, the rise of social and business networking sites has been phenomenal. MySpace started in 2002 and Facebook was founded in 2004. Facebook now has 200 million active users around the world. In the last two or three years, businesses have also grasped the opportunity.

Not only can you extend your reach through these sites, but you can also add a human face to your business. After all, people buy from people. Dell has 800,000 followers on Twitter, and they say that it has made a lot of money. The trick for any business that wants to use social networking sites is not to do a hard sell. Dell provides advice, tips and runs clinics. Everything is done in a light-hearted way. It does advertise, but in a low-key way and often in the form of money-off coupons.

There are seven reasons why you should embrace sites such as Twitter, Facebook, LinkeIn, MySpace and YouTube.

case study Twitter was launched in August 2006 and now has somewhere in the region of 50 million users around the world. It is the 30th biggest source of traffic on the Internet and

1 It will help you build relationships with potential customers and extend your reach around the world.

2 It acts like a viral marketing machine. People will tell their friends about you, your business and the things you say.

3 It will increase your brand awareness and what your brand stands for through what you say.

4 It shows that you are a leader and builds your credibility and trust. You can also use it to establish your business as a place of expertise in its field.

5 It will give you an insight into what people think about you and your business. Social networks are not one-way; people will comment on your business and the things you say.

6 It allows you to point people in the direction of more information on your blog or your website.

7 It is a way for you to discover new ideas and find opportunities to work with other businesses on joint ventures.

Don't ignore the power of social networking sites to get to markets you can't normally reach.

accounts for one in every 350 visits to other websites. Other great places for sources of Internet traffic are YouTube, Facebook and LinkedIn, the business networking site.

Make an achievable plan

This is the hardest thing for most marketing people to do, because they are doers rather than planners. But you do need to think about what you want to achieve and how you'll do it. Your plan doesn't have to be long, but it must be clearly thought through. You must also decide how to measure your progress. And, if it's not working as you planned, be flexible with your approach and honest enough to admit, "that didn't work, so let's try this instead."

7.1

Be clear about your ambition

Marketing people are innovators and doers, and this is probably the bit that most of them hate: writing it all down in a plan. But I can't stress enough the importance of spending some time on this. It helps to clarify your thoughts and explain to others what you plan to do and why.

Before you create your plan, you need to be very clear about your goal or your ambition. If you work in a large organization, this is probably your vision or mission statement, and it's usually something like, "to be the leading supplier of … in the world".

Smaller organizations express their goals in more direct ways. How many they want to sell, how much money they want to make, or how much market share they want. However, you must express it clearly so that everyone else understands what you're trying to do.

■ **Your goal.** This is what you want to achieve over the next 18 months to two years. No longer than this, as technology and markets move so fast these days. Think of something that you can easily measure in order to monitor your progress.

"A clear vision, backed by definite plans, gives a tremendous feeling of confidence"

Brian Tracy, motivational speaker and author

■ **Your strategies.** These are how you are going to achieve your goal. They could be things like: launch a new product, expand into a new area or start to sell products over the Internet.

■ **Your activities and objectives.** This is where you turn your strategies into tactics, or marketing activities. It includes exactly what you intend to do, who's going to do it and when it will be done.

■ **Your plan.** This explains the thinking behind your goals, strategies and activities. It also has a month by month activity plan and the financial justification for what you want to do.

The plan doesn't need to be very long, but it does need to contain some basic information. It should cover the Secrets that talk about your potential customers, your products and services, the places people will buy and how you will promote your business. It must also contain details of your main competition and a profit and loss statement. It does not usually need a cash flow analysis, although an investor might require that as well.

It's a drudgery, but your marketing plan is a keystone. It tells people not only what you're going to do, but also why you're going to do it.

7.2

Create a thorough long-term plan

Sometimes you have to prepare a full-blown marketing or business plan. This is not a short-term plan to launch a new product as in Secret 7.1, as it covers your business over the next three to five years.

This kind of plan must be an active document, so you must review it and update it every six to nine months. And you will have to add a bit on the end each time. A good plan helps you spot anything going wrong and allows you to do something about it. It also helps you to see areas that are going quicker or better than you had expected so you can exploit them. Your plan should be 20 to 30 pages long and must contain the following seven sections.

■ **Your goal.** Two or three pages, with the key points from the plan. Though it's at the front of the plan, you must write this last of all.
■ **Your products.** The description and pricing structure for each of your products and services. Plus any developments you intend to introduce over the time scale of the plan.
■ **Your market.** The definition, size and dynamics of your target markets. As well as the structure of your industry, the routes to market and details of your competitors.

> " The primary function of the marketing plan is to ensure that you have the resources and the wherewithal to do what it takes to make your business work "

Jay Levinson

■ **Your competitiveness.** The strengths and weaknesses of your business, and the opportunities and threats over the planning period. You must also state how you will exploit your strengths and opportunities and overcome your weaknesses and threats.

■ **Your approach.** How you are going to market and sell your products and services. Plus a forecast of sales volumes and values over the planning period.

■ **Your delivery plan.** How you intend to source, produce, provide and deliver your products and services. Include any additional resources that you will need.

■ **Your forecast.** A profit and loss forecast for each period in the plan, together with a cash flow forecast covering three years.

Your plan is a working document, so everybody understands what you intend to do and what resources you need. It should be clear, readable and honest. There is no point in building a business that's based on weak foundations.

Every business needs to understand where it wants to be in three to five years and how it will get there.

7.3

Always know how well you are doing

Just because you've got a plan, it doesn't necessarily mean that events will happen as you've mapped them out. Business is never that easy, and your competitors aren't going to ignore what you're doing. And the only way you can find out how well or badly things are progressing is to measure reality against your predictions and targets.

There are many marketing metrics, as they're called, and every company will have its own particular ways of doing things. However, I think that the first three on this list are mandatory.

■ **Monthly sales revenue and margin.** You must measure how much you sell and how much gross profit or sales margin you are making every month. Ideally, you should break this down further, and work out the figures for each of your products.

■ **Google Analytics.** You must install Google Analytics on your website so that you know how people found your site, what pages they looked at and how long they stayed.

one minute wonder Before you do your next promotional campaign, you must have a clear and measurable objective. Just "to promote a product" is not good enough. Make sure that you've put an action in the campaign, then measure how many people did what you wanted them to do.

■ **Campaign performance.** You must set an objective for every promotional activity, such as to increase awareness by 20% or generate 500 enquiries. If it's not working, stop it or revamp it.

■ **New customers.** Customers are the life blood of business. You must hold on to as many as you can, because it's cheaper to sell to someone who already knows you. Inevitably, though, you will lose some, so new customers are absolutely essential. Measure how many new customers you get each month, quarter and year.

■ **Customer satisfaction.** Bad news spreads fast, and a reputation for poor quality or bad service can take years to erase. You must talk regularly to your customers to find out what they think of you, your products and your service.

■ **Daily sales average.** If you run a shop or a business that has lots of customers, you must know how well you have done every day. Divide your annual target by the number of working days in the year to get a daily sales average.

The only way to tell whether your ideas are working is to measure them.

7.4

Not all customers are equal

It is a myth that all customers are equal. It's not just that they are different people, with different tastes and personalities, it's the fact that they spend different amounts of money. It costs you money every time you sell something to someone. The problem arises when that exceeds any potential profit that you would have made from the sale.

You must categorize your customers so that you understand which cost you money. Work out the sales by each customer over a period of time, such as a year. Put them into sales order, with the highest spenders at the top of your list. Calculate the cumulative sales, starting from the top of the list and working your way down until you reach the point where you have the customers that have generated 80% of your sales over the period. You will probably find that this is only 20% of your customers. This is called a Pareto analysis after the Italian Vilfredo Pareto, and is fairly standard across all businesses.

Let's call the customers who generated 80%, your regular customers. These are the ones that you must nurture, so they stay with you as they grow. What's interesting is that 20% of your regulars also generate 80% of the sales from the group. Let's call these your major customers. And you need to treat your major customers best of all. Some companies call them key customers, because they'll go out of business if they lose them.

The rest of your customers can be split into those that buy from you occasionally and those that have only ever bought once. You must decide whether you are going to spend your marketing money on them or not. If they've only bought once, they're probably not worth it.

■ **Major customers.** Treat them like royalty. If you start to lose them, you will probably go out of business. Give them preferential treatment and exceptional service. They're the ones you invite to play golf.

■ **Regular customers.** These generate the bread and butter of your business, and you need to look after them. Make sure they get good service and take note of anything they say about your business.

■ **Ad-hoc customers.** These buy from you every now and then. You probably don't want to lose them all, but you mustn't give them special treatment. Some will cost you more money than they generate.

■ **One-off customers.** These are people who have bought only once and are unlikely to buy from you again. Don't spend anything on them; their first sale probably cost you money anyway.

Some customers are more important than others and some are more trouble than they're really worth.

7.5

Don't be afraid to adjust your approach

In the first chapter we talked about the philosophy of marketing, and how marketing people love change because it brings opportunity. The reason you create a plan is to understand what you'll do to achieve your goal. The reason you measure everything is to know if things are going as you had planned.

Since a lot of marketing is a mix of guesswork and experience, you mustn't take it personally if things don't go quite as you intended. Be adult enough to say, "well, that didn't work, so let's try this". The ability to adapt to changing circumstances is one of the keys to successful marketing. Being able to make plans is important, but so too is being able to revise plans as things progress.

■ **Review what's happened.** Take time out to look at what you've done and assess how it's going. Be prepared to admit that things haven't gone as you'd thought, if that's the case.

■ **Modify your approach.** Stand back and think about what you could do to make your plans work. Or, come up with a new way to achieve the same objective.

■ **Adjust your plan.** Take your original plan and rework it. Look at the implications of changing your approach, and calculate the impact on your budget.

■ **Monitor and repeat.** Decide when you will look at how it's doing again. If it still isn't working, then you'll need to make a hard decision, ditch the idea and think of something else.

As a marketing person, you need an open mind and an inquisitive nature, so you notice what's going on in other businesses and industries. Become a power-user of the Internet, and watch what's going on in other countries. Subscribe to email newsletters, reports and marketing blogs, so you see what other people are doing. Good marketing people learn from their own mistakes and from the things that other people are doing.

Things don't always go as planned, so you must be adult enough to admit it didn't work as you thought.

Jargon buster

AIDA
The acronym marketing people use to help them create a promotion message. It stands for Attention, Interest, Desire and Action.

ATOM
see RSS

Benefit
What the feature of a product or service actually does for customers.

Brand
The identity or image of an organization or product of the organization. It is also the feeling that the organization's name and image creates in the customer's mind.

Buying stages
The mental stages that customers go through when they decide which product or service to buy. The four stages are: need or want, knowledge, preference, and buy and justify.

Channel
The chain of people and third parties that an organization uses to sell products and services to potential customers.

Competitive advantage
The perceived difference between an organization's offering and those of its competitors.

Drop-ship
To accept an order from a third party in a transaction, and supply the product and service to the customer direct.

Feature
The property or characteristic of a product or service.

Margin
The gross margin is the difference between the cost to make or buy-in a product and/or service and the selling price. The net margin is after the marketing and selling costs have also been subtracted.

Market
A group of potential customers for a particular type of product or product category.

Offering
What the customers experience when they buy a product or service from an organization. It's the product together with the customer service.

Outbound and inbound
These twin terms describe the direction of any customer communication. Outbound is something the company does to contact the customer (this could be a letter, email or phone call). Inbound is something the customer does to contact the company (a message on a website forum, for example).

Product life cycle

The term used to describe how the sales of a product vary over time. The product life cycle goes from introduction, through growth to eventual decline.

Profit

The margin left after all the costs of running the business have been subtracted from the gross margin.

Proposition

A short statement that says exactly what you do, for whom you do it and what they get out of it.

Push and pull

The terms used to describe how products are pushed through the channel through sales incentives, and how products are pulled through the channel by promoting them to potential customers.

Quantitative and qualitative

These are the two types of results you will get from a survey. Quantitative data refers to the numbers and qualitative data to the feelings and comments.

RSS and ATOM

These are automatic Internet feeds that will inform you when a blog or website has been updated with new information.

Segment

A smaller distinct section of a market that contains a group of customers with very similar characteristics.

Segmentation

The process whereby marketing people divide a market into smaller chunks, or segments.

Value

Price is what the customer pays, while value is what they think a product or service is worth.

Further reading

Books

Egan, John *Relationship Marketing*
(Prentice Hall, 2008)
ISBN 978-0273713197
Move from a company-centred business to
a customer-driven business.

Harding, Ford *Rainmaking*
(Adams Media, 2008)
ISBN 978-1598695885
A guide to marketing and selling profes-
sional services.

Jobber, David *Principles and Practice of
Marketing* (McGraw-Hill Higher Educa-
tion, 2006) ISBN 978-0077114152
The de-facto textbook for MBA students
and marketing undergraduates.

Kotler, Philip *Marketing Management*
(Pearson, 2008) ISBN 978-0131357976
The definitive book on classical marketing
techniques.

Levinson, Jay Conrad *Guerilla Marketing*
(Piatkus Books, 2007) ISBN 978-
0749928117) A classic that dramatically
changed marketing for small businesses.

McDonald, Malcolm *Marketing Plans*
(Butterworth-Heinemann Ltd, 2007)
ISBN 978-0750683869) The definitive
guide to preparing marketing plans.

Peppers, Don and Rogers, Martha *Return
on Customer* (Marshall Cavendish, 2005)
ISBN 978-1904879343 How to understand the true value and costs of customers.

Websites & blogs

http://marketing-expert.blogspot.com
A long-running blog, with on-line and
off-line marketing tips.#

http://sethgodin.typepad.com
A blog that's easy to read and has lots of
real-life marketing examples.

http://trendwatching.com
A website from one of the world's leading
trend-watching organisations.

www.searchengineworld.com
A blog with information on all the mainstream search engines and SEO techniques.

http://bloombergmarketing.blogs.com
A long-running and quirky blog that
concentrates on new media and social
networking.

http://blog.hubspot.com
A blog that covers all aspects of inbound
Internet marketing.

www.kksmarts.com/blog
A UK blog with advice, ideas and tips for
getting more traffic to your website.

www.affiliates4u.com/wiki/
A wiki from a UK company about affiliate
marketing and the industry.

www.nonprofitmarketingblog.com
A US blog dedicated to marketing in non-
profit organizations.

www.BusinessSecrets.net